IF YOU SPEAK IT, IT WILL COME

Plan A, B and C Alignment, Belief and Clarity
An A-Z Affirmation Journal

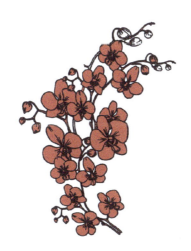

Mary Russell Hankins

Copyright © 2020 Mary Russell Hankins

All rights reserved. No part of this publication may be reproduced, distributed, or transmitted in any form or by any means, including photocopying, recording, or other electronic or mechanical methods, without the prior written permission of the publisher, except in the case of brief quotations embodied in reviews and certain other non-commercial uses permitted by copyright law.

Any internet addresses, phone numbers, company or product information printed in this book are offered as a resource and are not intended in any way to be or imply an endorsement by the publisher, nor does the publisher vouch for the existence, content, or services of these sites, phone numbers, companies, or products beyond the life of this book

ISBN 978-1-953194-91-6

Published by Believe In Your Book Publishing

Printed in the United States of America

For permission request, write to the publisher, addressed "Attention: Permissions Coordinator/ to the address below.

Email: BiybPublishing@gmail.com

IF YOU SPEAK IT, IT WILL COME

Plan A, B and C Alignment, Belief and Clarity

A-Z Affirmation Journal Belongs To:

Mr. Steve Harvey

Thank you for your encouragement and determination. You are my inspirational.

Thank you, Many Blessings upon you and your beautiful family.

Mrs. Mary Russell - Hankins

Dear Readers,

Thank you for purchasing this affirmation journal. I have written every page with your transformation in mind. I believe that you are reading this book because you are ready to make your own way. You are ready to take control of your life and no longer allow the actions of others to occupy a seat of authority over your circumstances. You are among the many people who desire to have transformative, life giving relationships.

In addition to practical steps, and explanations, I have shared my personal stories of
transformation, along with the tools that I used to find real change in my life. You will
find that my faith was instrumental in my transformation and earning freedom from the
suffering caused by faith to reach a point of no return. I feel so honored that you have
allowed me to travel with you on your journey to wholeness.

Now, let's get started.
Mary Russell Hankins
Mary Russell Hankins

About The Author

Mary Russell Hankins is the eldest of 3 siblings born and raised in Ft. Lauderdale, FL. to Prophet Donald Russell Sr. and Missionary Chantay Pinkney. She was raised in a well-known- respectable, educated Christian Family. Mary is an elect woman of God, wife and mother of four children only physically giving birth to one child. She attended Ely High School where she reached the 12th grade but unfortunately connected with the wrong crowd and didn't get the chance to graduate. She realized after having her child, she not only wanted to be a good mother but a greater example. She went back to school and received her Diploma.

Throughout the years "Faith, Family & Love", "And So Shall It Be Established" The newest addition "If you speak it, they will come" was birthed from a deep secret place inside Mary's heart. Her mind, spirit and heart was so dilapidated with hurt, pain and an emotional rollercoaster of disappointments. April 25th 2009, Mary made a vow to follow Christ no matter what or the cost. In that same year Mary's family suffered a serious near fatal tragedy, her husband was held at gunpoint, robbed and shot. Through her vow God healed her husband.

After that Mary soon began writing and in doing so, Mary realized the more she surrendered to God the more she began to gain wisdom, knowledge and understanding. Not fully realizing and knowing that if she had strong faith, she could have it all. Faith gave Mary strength to fight for her life as well as for her family. God envisioned Mary, to express her thoughts and expressions through her writing.

Mary has a passion for helping others win, in their lives but most of all their spiritual life. In spite of all her adversities, she continues to keep the faith and help as many individuals as she can who are in need of making any additional income with the opportunity of becoming their own boss.

Mary is a committed and loyal servant who loves God, her family and friends she has been sent to be an example to our future young ladies. She is an author who has written two other self help books; which entitles "Faith, Family & Love". "And So Shall It Be Established". Mary is not only a woman after Gods own heart but;

"She is a woman of Power, Purpose, Destiny and Faith."

DEDICATION

It is with deepest gratitude that I dedicate this book to God, my Lord and Savior.
For Encouragement and Love Beyond Measure
My husband Leonard
My children
My parents
My mother and father- in- law
My sister and brother
My loving and supportive family
My friends
Thank you for supporting me in all my endeavors.

- Blessings

IF YOU SPEAK IT, IT WILL COME

A Affirmation: the action or process of affirming something or being affirmed.

I am responsible for looking after me;
I am fine with who I am.
I will not accept anxiety.
I am not average.
I am the Apple of God's eye.
I command my angels to go before me daily.
I am anointed & appointed, equipped for the assignment.
I will put the word in action.

Jeremiah 1:15
Before I formed thee in the belly I knew thee; and before thou came forth out of the womb I sanctified thee, and I ordained thee a prophet unto the nations.

B

Bless: To confer or invoke divine favor upon; ask God to look favorably on.

I am a **Believer** therefore I will speak boldly.

I am about my Father's business therefore my natural business endeavors shall prosper.

I will bow down in worship to show my Father, that I believe & receive everything He has for me.

I will not have a bad attitude towards people, because I am born again.

I have faith to move mountains.

Mark 5:36
As soon as Jesus heard the word that was spoken, He saith unto the ruler of the synagogue, be not afraid, only believe.

IF YOU SPEAK IT, IT WILL COME

Change: Make or become different; transform.

Life is about making the right choices & once we realize that, we have power & authority,
to call those things as be not as though they were. Because it is He, who give me power to create wealth.
I command my angels to go before me.
I choose to change from my wicked ways.

Luke 4:10
For it is written, He shall give his angels charge over thee, to keep thee.

IF YOU SPEAK IT, IT WILL COME

D

Deliverance: the action of being rescued or set free.

**Today will be a great day.
I will speak positive.
I will not doubt nor fear.
I rebuke the spirit of depression & anxiety.
I will walk in full deliverance, so my light could shine
in dark places.
I speak it, I believe it, because life in death is in the power
of the tongue.**

**Psalms 118:24
This is the day which the Lord hath made; we will rejoice and be glad in it.**

E Encourage: give support, confidence or hope to (someone).

The number 8 represents new beginning, resurrection.
When you go into prayer & meditation, ask your Father
to open your spiritual ears so you may hear clearly, &
open your spiritual eyes, so you may see the vision for
your life.
I am strong in my new mindset.
I am brave enough to start new, in a new territory.
I will welcome new ideas & new surroundings.
Do not be afraid to exalt His name, whenever or wherever you are. For the wages of sin is death, but the
gift of God is eternal life in Christ Jesus our Lord.

2 Corinthians 5:17
(For we walk by faith, not by sight:)

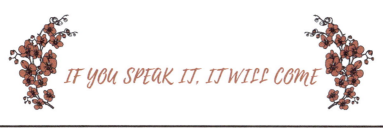
IF YOU SPEAK IT, IT WILL COME

F

Faith: complete trust or confidence in someone or something..

Now faith is the substance of things hoped for, the evidence of things not seen.
I will fight the good fight of faith.
I will lay hold on eternal life, where unto thou art also called, & hast professed a good profession before many witnesses.
I will praise thee; for I am fearfully and wonderfully made: marvelous are thy works; & that my soul knoweth right well.
I will walk in forgiveness.
Matthew 5:44 states "But I say unto you, love your enemies, bless them that curse you, do good to them that hate you, & pray for them which despitefully use you & persecute you."
I must forgive, so I can be forgiven.

Matthew 6:14
For if ye forgive men their trespasses, your heavenly Father will also forgive you:

IF YOU SPEAK IT, IT WILL COME

Grateful: feeling or showing appreciation of kindness; thankful.

I am so grateful that God is not a man that he should lie.
I am grateful that His grace is sufficient.
I am grateful because when I give, I give with a cheerful heart, good intentions.
I am grateful for the gifts & talents that have inside of me.
There are many gifts; wisdom, knowledge, faith & healing miracles & discernment of spirits, service & help.
What are your gifts?

Numbers 23:19

God is not a man, that he should lie; neither the son of man, that he should repent: hath he said, and shall he not do it? or hath he spoken, and shall he not make it good?

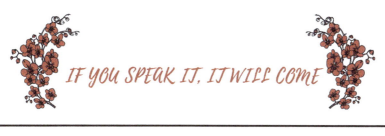

H

Heal: to become sound or healthy again.

In life, we all have experienced some hurts in our past. We've held on with an unforgiving heart which in turn causes us to have a lack of trust in people. Remember to be unforgiving doesn't hurt the other person, it only hurts you. It affects your spiritual growth & your physical health.
I will let the heaviness go.
I will walk in forgiveness & complete healing.
I will learn to trust again..

Psalms 37:4
Delight thyself also in the Lord: and he shall give thee the desires of thine heart.

IF YOU SPEAK IT, IT WILL COME

I

Increase: become or make greater in size, amount or degree to grow.

I declare & decree to increase in my mind, body & spirit.
I speak to increase in every area of my life and with that; I will increase in my personal life, increase in my finances, increase in my business, increase in my job.
I command promotion from the North, South, East and West.

Proverbs: 13:22
A good man leaves an inheritance to his children's children: and the wealth of the sinner is laid up for the just.

J

Joyful: Feeling, expressing, or causing great pleasure and happiness.

I will find joy.
I will be positive.
I will find myself in a place of happiness.
I will become full of laughter.
I will find inspiration, motivation & love.
I will dare myself to choose joy, smile & be merry.

Galatians 5:22
But the fruit of the Spirit is love, joy, peace, long-suffering, gentleness, goodness, faith.

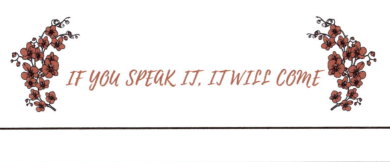

K kindness: the quality of being friendly, generous, and considerate..

Be kind to one another, forgive and be set free.
I will walk in peace, love & humility.
I will seek wisdom, knowledge & understanding.
I will not be weary in well doing.
Start by kneeling on your knees in prayer.
Arising in early morning in worship.
Praying for clarity, insight & vision.
Clear your mind, be slow to speak, follow your heart.

Galatians 5:22-23
But the fruit of the Spirit is love, joy, peace, long-suffering, gentleness, goodness, faith, meekness, temperance: against such there is no law.

IF YOU SPEAK IT, IT WILL COME

L

Love: an intense feeling of deep affection.

Love is a choice. Do not confuse love with expectations. Expectation is a strong belief that something will happen, or be the case i the future.

Love is a 4 Letter word.
L- life.
O-obedience,
V-victory
E-endurance.
I will choose love.
I will learn to walk in unconditional love without limitations.
I will celebrate love.
I will love unselfishly.

John 3:16
For God so loved the world, that he gave his only begotten Son, that whosoever believeth in him should not perish, but have everlasting life.

M

Mindset: is a collection of thoughts and beliefs that shape one's thoughts and habits.

I will rebuke the spirit of doubt & emotional manipulation.
I will rebuke negative thinking & negative speaking.
I will speak life into this situation at hand.
I will break free from worry.
I will trust the process.
May goodness & mercy will follow you all the days of your life.
May you witness miracles that will shock your natural eyes.

Matthew 24:4
And Jesus answered and said unto them, take heed that no man deceives you.

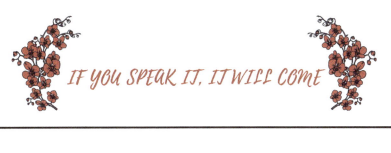

IF YOU SPEAK IT, IT WILL COME

Necessary: required to be done, achieved, or present; needed; essential.

**Everything you have been through or going through, is & was necessary.
Don't be afraid to upgrade your testimony, because your 'yes' isn't about you.
Your yes is about the individuals you're going to be assigned too.
Think it not strange, don't pray for an exit, pray for endurance
to complete the assignment.
I will find the strength to forge ahead.
I will find the courage to say 'yes'.
I will be selfless in my acts.**

1 Peter 5:10
But the God of all grace, who hath called us unto His eternal glory by Christ Jesus, after that ye have suffered a while, make you perfect, stablish, strengthen, settle you.

O Obedience: complying or willing to comply with orders or requests; submissive to another's will.

Walking in obedience, & asking God to search your heart, brings you in to a spiritual alignment.
I will walk in obedience.
I will reject instant gratification
I will search my heart & carefully reflect upon my own emotions & motivations for something.
I will let God guide the way.

Psalms 139:23
Search me, O God, and know my heart: try me, and know my thoughts:And see if there be any wicked way in me and lead me in the way everlasting.

IF YOU SPEAK IT, IT WILL COME

Process: A series of actions or steps taken in order to achieve a particular end.

The roads of peace, happiness & love lead you on the path of transition. This is very important, because it brings the focus you need to make things better. As you embrace change, people may walk out your life. You may be rejected from close family & friends. When you trust the process, you will see your growth.
I will trust.
I will believe.
I will stay focused.
I will grow.

Psalms 56:3
What time I am afraid, I will trust in thee.

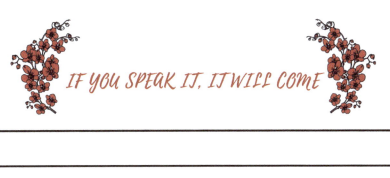
IF YOU SPEAK IT, IT WILL COME

Quiet: making little or no noise. carried out discreetly, secretly, or with moderation.

When facing hardships, it's necessary to find a quiet space to gather your thoughts and find peace in your mind. When you find yourself falling into the spirit of heaviness, go to your quiet place, or space.

I will become one with my thoughts.
I will find a peace of mind.
I will find my balance.
I will release this weight on my shoulders.

Psalms 91:1
He that dwelleth in the secret place of the most High shall abide under the shadow of the Almighty.

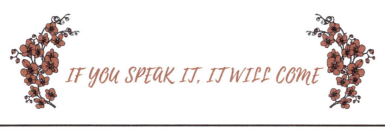

IF YOU SPEAK IT, IT WILL COME

Relationships: The way in which two or more concepts objects or people are connected.

There are many different types of relationships but what makes a good relationship?

A good relationship is an ability to communicate effectively. Once you know & love yourself, you're better able to express yourself with integrity.

I will be happy.
I will be vulnerable.
I will be honest.
I will be my authentic self.

Matthew 6:33
But seek ye first the kingdom of God, and his righteousness; and all these things shall be added unto you.

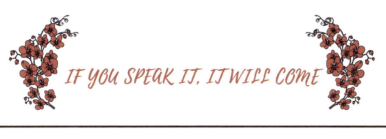
IF YOU SPEAK IT, IT WILL COME

S

Strength: the quality or state of being physically strong.

Life is about sowing, or planting, seeds. Seeds of encouragement, seeds of joy and happiness.
What does it mean to sow seeds? Figuratively speaking, you can also sow things like doubts or ideas, simply by spreading them around. If your ideas (or your seeds) develop and grow, you've successfully sown them.
I am strong.
I am confident.
I am able.
I choose happiness.
I will continue to grow.
What seeds are you planting?

Luke 8:4-18;
"And when a great crowd was gathering and people from town after town came to him, he said in a parable: "A sower went out to sow his seed. And as he sowed, some fell along the path and was trampled underfoot, and the birds of the air devoured it.

T

Truth: the quality or state of being true.

Take time to be refreshed & refueled. Without vision, we become unbalanced & unstable. It is important to rewrite the vision, pray & fast to gain clarity for the next season.
I will trust the process.
I will seek wisdom because the truth will set me FREE.

John 8:32
And ye shall know the truth, and the truth shall make you free.

Understand: Perceive the intended meaning of words, a language, or speaker.

When you love unconditionally, you are choosing to love someone in their entirety. We are not perfect and neither is whom we love. Acknowledge and lean on God to show you the way.
I understand no one is perfect.
I understand that not everything is for me.
I will accept people for who they are and show me to be.
I will lean on God to direct my path

Proverbs 3:5-6
Trust in the Lord with all thine heart; and lean not unto thine own understanding. In all thy ways acknowledge him, and he shall direct thy paths.

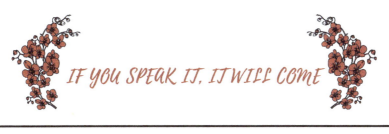

IF YOU SPEAK IT, IT WILL COME

V

Victory: An act of defeating an enemy or opponent in a battle, game or other competition.

Repeat: Victory is mine, Victory is mine.
I am in my right mind.
I have faith in the test.
I know that I'm blessed.
In the midst of the storms, I am equipped to hold on.
I am blessed, I am blessed, in all things, I am blessed.
Victory is mine, I shall WIN every time.

Ephesian 6:13
Wherefore take unto you the whole armor of God, that ye may be able to withstand in the evil day,
and having done all, to stand.

W

Wisdom: having experience, knowledge & good judgment; the quality of being wise.

Wisdom is knowing when and how to use your knowledge.
I will be decisive when the right decisions appear before me.
I will be mindful.
I am healthy, wealthy & wise.
I will deal with all problems that torment me with wisdom and grace.
I will use my knowledge and wisdom to better understand.

Proverbs 4: 6-7
Do not forsake Wisdom, and she will protect you; love her and she will protect: Wisdom is Supreme; therefore get wisdom. Though it cost all you have, get understanding.

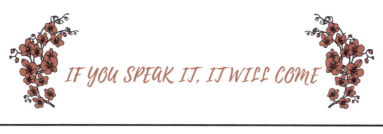

IF YOU SPEAK IT, IT WILL COME

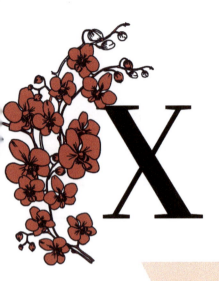

X

Exit: a way out, especially of a public building, room, or passenger vehicle.

I will walk in fullness.

I will follow God's way of escape from any situation that may cause me harm.

I will not be tempted beyond my own or others capabilities.

1 Corinthians 10:13
No temptation has overtaken you except such as is common to man; but God is faithful, who will not allow you to be tempted beyond what you are able, but with the temptation will also make the way of escape, that you may be able to bear it.

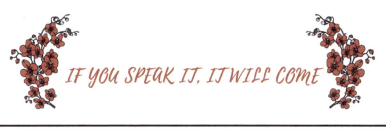

Y

Yes: used to give an affirmative response.

Your yes, isn't about you. Your YES is about the people, that will be assigned for you. Your assignment will be to help & serve on your journey.
I will be willing and open to serve.
I will guide with the words of the Lord.
I will help those in need. I will put the word in action.

Matthew 5:37
But let your 'Yes' be 'Yes' and your 'No' be 'No.' Whatever is more than these is of the evil one.

Zeal: great energy or enthusiasm in pursuit of a cause or an objective.

Having zeal can contribute to your success. Hard work and determination is the energy from which dreams are made! You must be passionate, have love & fire to succeed.

I am willing.
I am energized & motivated.
I am passionate about my convictions.
I stand firmly in love.
I am determined to pursue my dreams and goals.
I will begin this day with great energy and enthusiasm.
I am successful.

Romans 10:2
For I bear them record that they have a zeal of God, but not according to knowledge.

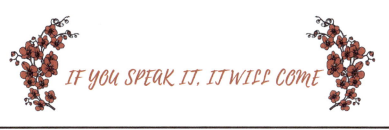

IF YOU SPEAK IT, IT WILL COME

IF YOU SPEAK IT, IT WILL COME

IF YOU SPEAK IT, IT WILL COME

IF YOU SPEAK IT, IT WILL COME

IF YOU SPEAK IT, IT WILL COME

IF YOU SPEAK IT, IT WILL COME

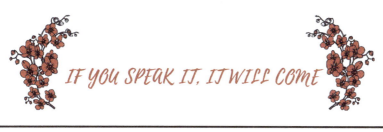

IF YOU SPEAK IT, IT WILL COME

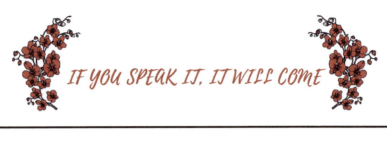

IF YOU SPEAK IT, IT WILL COME

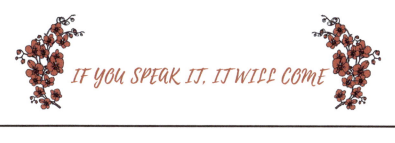
IF YOU SPEAK IT, IT WILL COME

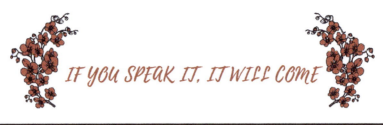
IF YOU SPEAK IT, IT WILL COME

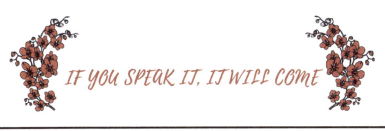

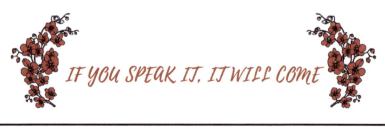
IF YOU SPEAK IT, IT WILL COME

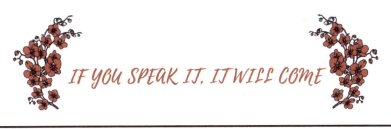

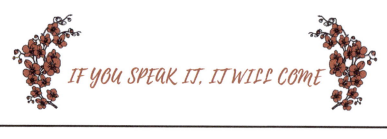

IF YOU SPEAK IT, IT WILL COME

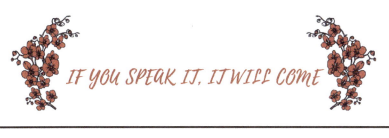

IF YOU SPEAK IT, IT WILL COME

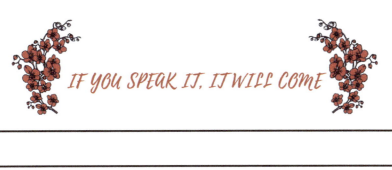

IF YOU SPEAK IT, IT WILL COME

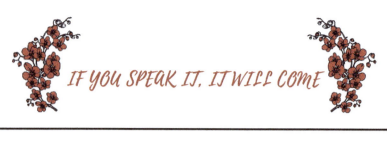

IF YOU SPEAK IT, IT WILL COME

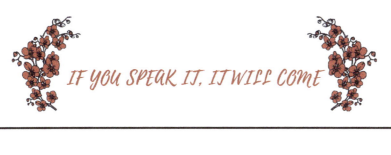
IF YOU SPEAK IT, IT WILL COME

IF YOU SPEAK IT, IT WILL COME

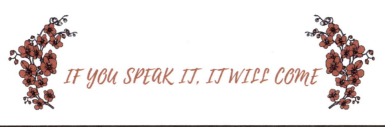

IF YOU SPEAK IT, IT WILL COME

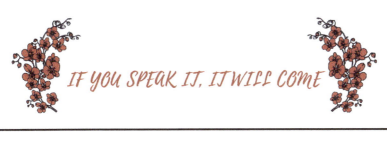
IF YOU SPEAK IT, IT WILL COME

IF YOU SPEAK IT, IT WILL COME

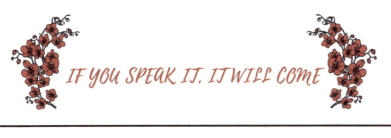
IF YOU SPEAK IT, IT WILL COME

IF YOU SPEAK IT, IT WILL COME

IF YOU SPEAK IT, IT WILL COME

IF YOU SPEAK IT, IT WILL COME

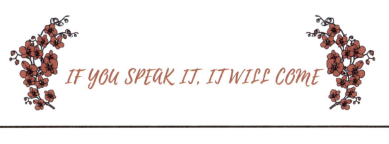
IF YOU SPEAK IT, IT WILL COME

IF YOU SPEAK IT, IT WILL COME

IF YOU SPEAK IT, IT WILL COME

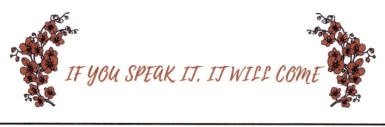

IF YOU SPEAK IT, IT WILL COME

IF YOU SPEAK IT, IT WILL COME

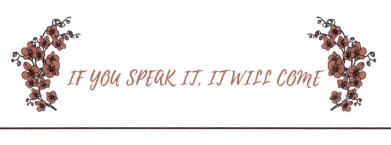

IF YOU SPEAK IT, IT WILL COME

IF YOU SPEAK IT, IT WILL COME

IF YOU SPEAK IT, IT WILL COME

IF YOU SPEAK IT, IT WILL COME

IF YOU SPEAK IT, IT WILL COME

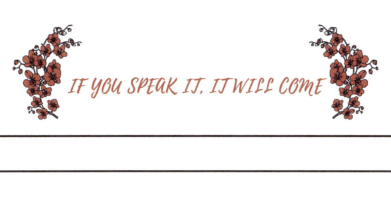
IF YOU SPEAK IT, IT WILL COME

IF YOU SPEAK IT, IT WILL COME

CPSIA information can be obtained
at www.ICGtesting.com
Printed in the USA
LVHW071102310721
694190LV00006B/76